NEW STARS &
CONSTELLATIONS
DAVID CAZDEN

Bainbridge Island Press

NEW STARS &

CONSTELLATIONS

DAVID CAZDEN

Bainbridge Island Press
Bainbridge Island, WA

Published in 2024 by Bainbridge Island Press
Bainbridge Island, WA
https://bainbridgeisland.press

Printed in the United States of America

ISBN: 978-1-961451-06-3
Library of Congress Control Number: 2024945211

Cover & Book Design: Ben Rockwood
Editor: Tamarah Rockwood

9 8 7 6 5 4 3 2 1

To My Brother, Gene

ACKNOWLEDGEMENTS

I'm grateful to the editors of the following magazines where these poems, often in their original form, first appeared or are forthcoming.

The New Republic	"Boyle County Snake"
The Shore	"As A Child, I Hold A Mercury"
	"Thermometer Under My Tongue"
Fare Foreward	"Arboreal Sketch"
The McNeese Review	"In The 80s"
Canary	"Feral Dogs Of Chernobyl"
Barely South Review	"A Kentucky Goodbye"
Susurrus	"Perfume," "The Tides"
Rust + Moth	"Pathways"
Amethyst Review	"Moving Colors"
The Sunlight Press	"Child Of The Sun"
South Florida Poetry Journal	"In The 70s"
Still: The Journal	"Elegy For Lyn Lifshin"
The Heartland Review	"Ice Storm 2021"
Valparaiso Poetry Review	"Vertigo"
Anti-Heroin Chic	"My First Job," "Shadow"
The Write Launch	"Mystic Owl," "Vines"
Passages North	"Divination At A Hilltop Cemetery,"
	"When You Were A Librarian" [1,3]
The Louisville Review	"Feeding The Ospreys" [2]
Fugue Journal	"Border Drive" [1,3]
Apple Valley Review	"Portrait Of Time As An Old Woman" [1]
Stirring	"Your Organic Garden" [2]
Heavy Feather Review	"In The Dark"
Salvation South	"Called Home," "Stream"
Rattle	"The Joy Of Cooking School" [2]
Samsarra	"To My Masseuse" [2]
Kestrel	"December Arabesque" [1]
Crab Creek Review	"Indricotherium" [1]
Poetry South	"Things I Keep Near"

1—An earlier version of this poem appeared in *The Lost Animals* (Sundress Publications, 2013)
2—An earlier version of this poem appeared in *Moving Picture* (Wordtech, 2005)
3—Anthologized by Glass Lyre Press, in *Aeolian Harp*, 2023

CONTENTS

I

II

III

IV

V

NEW STARS & CONSTELLATIONS
DAVID CAZDEN

I

A KENTUCKY GOODBYE

1981

By the time I saw you
in skirts of jasmine
and sweaters of dandelions,
it was almost too late.
We were in college
rounding a hill to summer,
taking a gentle slope down.
Then on a day by a pond
we watched dragonflies hover,
measuring distances—shore to horizon,
reed to water lily, sunlit rock
to wisp of brown hair.
Something was being calculated
beginning to end.
We talked, tossed rocks,
braved mosquitoes
fine as newsprint
on the way to the car.

After driving to your apartment,
we watched Jason Robards in *1000 Clowns*
and took angel dust
which made the lights shimmer.
We could smell fruit
off night-blooming trees
and the lavender scarf
of the wind. You told me
you were leaving, as the angel
dust settled like dusk
in the pond behind us,
filling our footsteps, sifting
down strip-mined hills
on grass soft as catsfur, clinging
with this restless glow
we still feel
in the hollows and valleys
in the lines of our hands.

FERAL DOGS OF CHERNOBYL

World's worst nuclear accident, 1986

Radiation lurks invisibly
appearing only in pictures
on old fashioned film—
flashing like apparitions
in videos of abandoned schoolrooms,
over hastily dropped dolls
and dust covered shoes.
For earth never stays still,
licking its own wounds
of poison rivers, stunted meadows
and mutated fields.
Yet somewhere, paws plow in dirt,
insect antennae probe wavelengths
of tainted air. And the children
of the children of the children
of our abandoned pets remain.

Science thinks they're evolving faster,
that their DNA's mutating more
and perhaps they won't howl
at sickle moons
or keen in shrunken forests
that inexplicably turned red
where they dart shadow to shadow.
Living only three years,
each generation renews
the way all feral pets do—
When an invisible thread
tears from the womb,
unraveling a hole in space,
where the pups crawl through
onto the ground, somehow
made new, yet different,
fallen stars all around them.

CAT'S CRADLE

We found her in a shelter,
infected with *herpes felis*.
She never breathed easy,
sneezing on walls, leaving tears
like blood stained petals
on the pillow.
Yet she sleeps by my head
with crusty eyes that still gleam
emerald, even in daylight—
and pupils thin as splintered
midnight sky. Because she follows us
room to room, house to house,
we name her Shadow.
Whenever we lie down,
Shadow crawls between us.
Sometimes I drift away
to her wheezing breath,
my hand on her coat,
its deepening softness
without beginning or end
and I'll think of my brother,

OD'd at 35—of us as kids
playing in the yard,
sun dipping in the hollies.
Then the clarity of burial day
in an old growth cemetery,
leaves and seedpods at our feet.
And I feel the bed turn in orbit
with the clockwork planets
and flywheel moon, keeping time
as they did at our old house—
where below shedding oaks
and peeling gutters
we left our footsteps.
Sometimes I forget
to clean Shadow's face
and eyes with saline—
She pulls back, stretching
in a feline curve, dark
fur spilling on the sheets
from the bed's faint edge
to the slip of dawn.

LA TABACON

Costa Rica, 1991

We sleep near riches—
jewels of bromeliads
strung like bracelets
on wrists of strangler figs—
petals cupped to rain
holding poison dart frogs eggs.
At La Tabacon
we wake early
to clucks and songs
of oropendola, howler monkcys
bellowing, curdling the dawn.
The window blinds
of our small wood hut
throw patterns
of sun and forest shadow,
mimicking a jaguar's coat
we barely see in dreams.

At La Tabacon
we wash the morning down
with pungent coffee,
sugar cane cut fresh
by the machete,
cream from nearby farms.
Outside, Lake Arenal
kneels at the mountain's feet.
By dusk we see its cinders spew
from beneath the continent,
tumbling down each evening's slope.
After we fly home,
the rainforest doesn't leave.
It exhales oxygen into our pores.
And sometimes the jaguar
stalks the perimeter of our sleep
as Mt. Arenal throws sparks,
lighting up the path we made
so long ago, into the jungle night.

PATHWAYS

We shared a hymnal,
pulling a pink ribbon
through gilt-edged pages
where our fingers touched.
The congregation's mouths
formed 'o's as everyone
inhaled at once, voices
echoing in the neighborhood.
We snuck out early. Nearby houses
wore sweaters of thick rain,
the grass was slick with moldy leaves,
black walnuts rocked beneath our feet.
We tripped into a nearby park—
under catalpas
where neighbors sat and read
in a corner of late autumn.

At sixteen, it was my second time
or my third. It did not seem
superfluous—not with cold
rain fine as sand, leaves
twirling on thin stems.
Perhaps I knew, as car lights
shined in our clothes—
spirits followed us.
Cement-gray clouds pulled like silk
over bare nightsky,
revealing all light's pathways,
new stars and constellations
burned into our skin.

OUR DOG

Looking through the living room window
at every squirrel darting

in sun-bent limbs, our dog appears,
as much as a dog can,

to hold his breath,
as if he can't believe what he's seeing.

Perhaps he thinks
of early morning bird chatter,

branches rubbing, footsteps
of apples falling. When the consonants

of autumn intrude in his sleep,
he'll twitch his paws like he's running,

releasing a muted cry
from his side of the bed.

He watches squirrels trace figure-eights
beneath burning locks of goldenrod,

squirrels spinning circles
through a choir of sunflowers

and though he's shown restraint so far,
when I crack the door, he bolts

bounding up and howling.
For a moment, he's no longer ours

but belongs to the quilt
of yellow and russet leaves

thrown across the shoulders
of the hills, in Indian summer,

weaving in thatched light
toward the creatures of his dreams.

MOVING COLORS

At an exhibit by Grace Walker Goad, autistic artist of Nashville.

The color pink unfolds
over her painting, a hue
like two vinyl gloves
I wore cleaning my parents' house
before it was sold—
pink as our living room window
mirroring early spring buds
where, drapes buttoned up,
a scarf of wind on the chimney,
Mom sat in winter
in yellow lamplight.
Another painting's the color
of our 70s kitchen
in marigold-yellow,
like wild mustard
staining hills behind our backyard
or Mom's blouse filling with sun
when she opened the windows
to wake me.

Because the painter's autistic
"with a lack of muscle control,"
she paints only abstracts—
Everything's communicated
through shape and hue
and swaths of sheer color.
I try to imagine
the artist's hand
opening over the canvas
the first time, like being born
again in the sky—
For it's possible
to be born over and over.
And as I stroll down the gallery hall
I am filled up with color
as if it were spirit,
before taking the concrete steps
to the parking lot—
into cool air,
under familiar stars
in the late light of a blue moon.

ARBOREAL SKETCH

With luck, as the trees
hold pages of light
in outstretched limbs

I manage another day—
touching the smooth white skin
of the stove

blinking away shards of sleep.
The pale countenance of the drapes
shines in the bare room

while through the window
each leaf paints its shadow
on a neighbor's mildewed roof.

Then the hiss of tapwater,
whir of a coffee grinder
and my cat purring

gems of sound
as she pads the dim lit floor
where we once walked.

The study window
presents an alternate view—
where I stare absently, writing

a name on my palm
as the pen spills ink like twilight
scented by earth

over my life line
so by the time I look up—
it's halfway to noon.

The kettle's bare, cat's sleeping,
dew's drying on the eaves—
each drop large enough

to mirror the oaks
spanning the neighborhood,
holding all of my thoughts

on their curved surface,
tinted yellow and green
like your hazel eyes.

II

AS A CHILD, I HOLD A MERCURY THERMOMETER UNDER MY TONGUE

Then it drops, glass breaking,
quicksilver scattering
like mirrored ball bearings.
Trying to hold it,
it slips through my hands
and I feel like Mom
trying to keep a thought
after age 50. I imagine
a substance like mercury
follows me wherever I go—shining
on staircases, pooling in plane aisles.
Returning home, I glimpse it
on gray tile floors,
slipping through keyholes
where thoughts often leave
a nursing home's doors.
The night Mom passes, I dream
she's rummaging in the house,
rearranging sheets, blankets,
pinning up laundry
as my shirts and pants flutter
in the shape of a body.
I wake up wishing
we are still at Coos Bay
off the Oregon coast
in August's isthmus of heat—
Sunlight hits the waves,
cascading down rocks
into smooth surf
holding all our reflections,
glinting them back to the sky.

DIVINATION AT A HILLTOP CEMETERY

Frankfort, Kentucky, overlooking the Kentucky River,
near the grave of Major John Bibb, developer of Bibb lettuce.

I watch vultures trace ellipses
with the compasses of wings,
dropping down a thousand foot

gorge, above misted water.
Across, a few houses,
smudged dark with coal smoke

slump into a hillside.
What a place to live,
near a mouth of earth

formed into a single vowel,
full of fog and spirits
and so steep and quiet

only a deer could clamber down.
Any animal would be at home
in this still place, nibbling

moss off headstones,
ambling to the river
through a scrim of stunted shrubs.

And its hooves, ankles, fur
might glow in the sunlight
the way Major Bibb's hands

must have, holding
that first hybridized lettuce—
broad leaves veined

with yellow mist, its taste
full, like the gorge's depths.
And after chewing that sweet leaf's

flesh, perhaps Major Bibb
understood
the secret of these distances

where the dead linger
and animals wander hungry—
teeth, hooves and fur

permanently stained
by a mystery in green.

FAIRY TALE CEMETERY

My brother and I sip porridge,
the kind served
only in fairy tales
with the melted butter
and milk of childhood.
I spy one wiry bear hair
spiraling under his tunic
but say nothing as Mom works
at the sink by the window.
Here honeybees
weave over the lawn,
sewing flowers from the ground
into the drapes, pulling and knotting
violets, daises,
a pink iris Mom planted
and all the violet wild grasses.
Soon there's only bare dirt,
a few pebbles like headstones
for creatures with no blooms
to feed them. Years later, returning,

I check the cold iron stove,
stacked porridge bowls,
dry wooden spoons,
half hoping to see steam
rising from the iron pot
or sink water splashing down.
But where the needlepoint
of our yard meets the asphalt,
my brother scampered
into the wild woods
where bears often return
who die young.
Perhaps the drapes, dense
with intertwined flowers,
dimmed Mom's view
as her memory left—
as if the bees flew
missions of kindness,
keeping out stark daylight
and bright fairy tale nights.

MYSTIC OWL

After the painting by Sabra Crockett, "The Mystic"

At dusk, a barn owl
puts on a riding coat
of gray-white feathers
and mounts a horse of air.
Galloping away,
he brings silent death
to mice and voles
in fields beside our farm.
Once full, he tugs the reins
of gravity, and the horse
pulls across our yard
to a favorite branch
on an ancient cherry tree.
Perched, the owl meditates
in metallic starlight
on the night-black trunks
of cherry, oak, blighted elm.
The owl's mystic temple
is this latticework of branches
where he turns the two
round disks around each eye
collecting faintest sounds—
distant rain, heartbeats
of robins tucked in nests,
rabbits rustling in warrens.

He makes one last flight
above the sparkling creek,
across the cool dark meadow,
guiding his invisible steed
into the barn, where he hangs
his gray-white coat
across a weathered door
like a broken patch of sun.
Another dawn. We awaken,
water cattle, scatter hay.

We hardly ever see
the owl, except in paintings
or in dreams. So we bend
in our daily chores,
knowing he lives nearby,
which somehow makes us happy
as we work into the day,
trying to be wise.

FEEDING THE OSPREYS

Working at the Osprey Reintroduction Project at the Rockcastle
River, 1993.

This is the view we sought
when we volunteered—
peering through a cage

above the ground
across a river's griddle of flat water,
watching ospreys tear

fish heads from a bucket
swinging from your arm.
We cling to a pull down ladder

through a mesh of evergreens.
Amid raptor-reek and soggy straw
carrion beetles

rush from hollows in the wood,
each with a morsel of fish
scuttled between the slats.

This is the final day
atop the rickety ladder
dangling from the lair,

the last glimpse
of hooded eyes
peering back so steadily

it could be ourselves,
gazing at each other
in the dark.

We let the door swing free
to a surge of feathers
rising up like fast water.

It's difficult to leave
birds hand-fed for a year.
So we watch them trace the ribs

of cirrus clouds—so full of hunger
they almost disappear
above the quickening waves.

CHILD OF THE SUN

Once the sun kissed you
to a blush-red shade.
Now a doctor

covers incisions
with balms and gauze, soft
as the haze over broken roofs

and crooked trees
of our neighborhood.
Perhaps you remember—

we crept on the lawn
past mushrooms throwing
spores fine as stars.

Similarly, I release
prayers toward your bed,
but you're still as sculpture

on pillows and sheets,
tucked like a passage
in a hymnal.

We're still entangled
where honeysuckle winds
on weathered fences

gutters sip rain
and pine needles drift
from the eaves.

Perhaps we never left—
As morning glories climb
a garden lattice, clinging

tight as shirts over ribs,
our neighborhood waits
for our steps, a few blocks

from the hospital,
where familiar clouds build
disperse, build again.

Growing up, the seasons
gathered this way, turning to rain
in your gray eyes.

THE JOY OF COOKING SCHOOL

She was involved in complexities of shallots.
He peeled thin skins, parting a garlic clove
like a dancer's pale shoes.
At break time they spooned milk froth
over espressos.

Their talk was euphoric,
young faces flushed
Renoir-red
in spirals of steam.

They wondered where it would lead,
the smearing of flour
into the fat of a lamb,
the coaxing of spices

into a quiche.
Then graduation —
hair wilted with oil
tucked into apprentice chef's caps.
They toiled in a stainless steel kitchen,
coming home late, heavy-headed.

At night they learned to be young—
spilled food on the floor,
laughed when they broke
a capon's hollow bones
or cracked eggs in a pan

into the mad hours
with nothing better to do
than beat cream into peaks,
let shy thyme and dill
grow amorous under the moon.

YOUR ORGANIC GARDEN

Late at night you drown
earwigs off the daisies,
holding them with tweezers
underwater.
You run your hands
along the plants
and anything that pinches back
get crushed, buried in a glass.
You reach beneath the dill,
eggplant and the spinach—
soft, broad leaves
flat against the ground
like hats of tropical
plantation owners wives—
But in a humble garden
you're no more sinister
than any other woman
with a flashlight, a pair of tweezers
and a jar of drifting wings.
One afternoon we even watch
a Purple Swallowtail hatch—
its velvet body vibrates
wet from the cocoon,
crawling up the vine,
as you bend
back all the stems
just to reach the air.

BOYLE COUNTY SNAKE

In Danville's quiescent morning
my neighbor knocked
"I'm Ebony from next door,
I found a snake
and if my husband ever knows
he'll sell our place and move away."
I wanted to help
so I took my snow shovel
into summer, and Ebony and I
went behind the house.
Wild, new grass—
tough contractor's mesh
on the fledgling lawn
where I found a five foot snake
beneath the nets.
Now I knew, in Boyle county, snake
eyes slit like vertical blinds
meant venom, days of pain,
that round eyes
reflect only our own fear
and the faintest rinds of sky.

So I made five shovel stabs
just to break the mesh
and lift the net away.
I cradled the serpent on the shovel,
its mouth opening as if to speak,
body coiling in memory's thickets.
I carried it to a field of copper grasses
that seemed to stretch forever
behind our homes.
I hoped it would survive
thin as a thread of moonlight
in the rippling fields.
Walking home,
my morning returned
with that stillborn silence
only small towns have.
Late afternoon clouds plumed in,
unfolding like a spell.

Rains knocked our town,
fattening rings of trees, washing
everything—loose grass, slivered scales
and all the poison we imagined—
not the shame we felt,
putting plastic on the lawns,
trapping whatever clings
beside us on the ground.

BORDER DRIVE

For R.S., R.I.P. 2010, by her own hand.

As I drive, each barn, cow,
bridge and silo

makes a wake of sound.
Bunchgrass hums

sheets of summer wheat
shudder.

Then, settling pools, cisterns,
hay-bales, spools

of bailing wire, all pass—
unwound from wooden shafts,

the wire gleams like a nerve,
knotted into fences, binding

the wheat in sheaves—
and in roadside furrows

they wait, as you must have,
to transform

to dust—to flour and husk—
in harvest light.

On an overpass from Des Moines
I close the windows and imagine you

buying that tank of helium,
filling your lungs' balloons

breathing in
until the string pulled from your hand.

You left without a note,
no words expanding

among the peaks and troughs
which form the tones

of a landscape,
where each object passing

plucks the air around my car
—as if to exist

is to make sound,
to speak or to be spoken for.

IN THE 60S

Fevers blew through me
like static on the t.v.
as I curled in bed.
Ghostly figures spoke
but I only listened—
to *Dark Shadows*
or Walter Cronkite's voice,
smooth as water over stones.
When the fever's caul
lifted from my sleep,
it left welts and swellings.
In middle school
I paid attention
when they told us we'd go metric,
that there wouldn't be enough food
so people might fall
off the edge of the world.
As teen, I blurred in and out
of our side screen door,
to the car or backyard path—
leaving footprints in the crabgrass
where, having sex the first time,
seemed easy as unbuttoning algebra,
until the moon of her
stuck beneath my skin—
glowing, throbbing,
waxing and waning over the years.

And like all the 60s,
there was no beginning or end.
When Mom contracted dementia,
I could see in every summer
another autumn—maple seeds
twirling down beside our house
catching in the window screens
as the screen door opened, closed—
shrieking and clamoring,
complaining to the wind.

IN THE 70S

No one was shot
at Henry Clay high school.
Instead, we died on the road.
At first, a sudden skid
you couldn't pull out of,
then a fusion of metals—
chrome with red paint,
Ford and Chevy, a nova
of glass, and the scent
of booze evaporating
like wraiths to the afterlife.
If you didn't flip a car,
you might flip from drugs.
When I took acid
for the week my parents were gone,
every surface
was embellished in reptile scales—
Cars slithered past, engines hissed,
lizards curled in the sheets.

I slept in thistles
until it wore off
like house paint.
Layers of myself
peeled away
with the fall leaves—
russet-gold, yellow-gold—
blowing over roads
into winter's coat. In the 70s,
Mom stopped driving
and didn't leave the house.
Her m.s. was worse.
Our food, odorless, tasted
of overcast skies. Time
sloughed away
like frozen pears
on the branches.
My bother left home
and Dad fell on the stairs,
tumbling like fruit in autumn.

When I finally left,
acorns fell from limbs,
whole forests tucked
in their endosperms—
brown hulls cracking
over the sidewalks,
crumbling and bending
with the world
under my feet.

IN THE 80S

We were tinted
by disco lights,
flashing cinnabar, jade.

Our drinks were tipped with sugar,
a twist of mint
like an arm around our waists.

Our faces glinted
bright as streaks of obsidian
on cliffs of a dance room floor

when you plucked the shine
from a Kentucky evening,
sprinkling it like glitter

on your lips and eyes.
When we went home
you kicked off tourmaline shoes

and in a decade of Ska,
mescaline, Castañeda,
the bathwater ran vermilion—

winds rolled over mesas,
derechos and siroccos
rippled in valleys

and deserts of our bodies
and we lost our names
like skiffs upon the waves.

By the time we split
the decade passed
and the dance without steps

the incantation of the bath
and dance hall cliffs, fell to shadows
and rippling sand.

TO MY MASSEUSE

Thumbs in, she presses on my spine,
her hands tracing its slow turns,
down the sore, potholed road,

up the bony steps, around the rusted gate,
to the backyard grass.
She is so young, I hide

undressed, face down
in the massage mattress.
She pulls nettles

in the neglected muscles,
kneads holly berries
underneath the skin.

Adhesions, she explains,
deep among thickened boughs
dense with swirls, fibers

tangled up
like kite string
unreeled in a storm.

For this I place a tip on the counter,
as a relaxation tape
unwinds beside a bottle

of evening primrose oil.
She stays in the other room
when I dress, body open
like a new moon.

AT LAKE HERRINGTON PIER

We weave a conversation,
unraveling threads of childhood clothes.
We unspool my jacket
and your old blue jeans.
You throw your shawl
across a chair—tinged
with melancholy colors—
stale sunsets, fallow fields,
gray shuttered barns.
You wear it on your arms
as we splash the water's surface
of stars and sodium lamps,
our reflections fracturing
into silty shallows
where herons stalk
on spindly legs.
We choose our words carefully,
the way streams pick twigs—
in rolling mouths,
traveling for miles
until they put their burden down
on murky banks. That night
I don't care about your shawl
of moody weather
draped across your shoulders,
cuffs dangling like dusk
into the mountains—
For it's only you and I
watching nighthawks swoop
insects off the wing
as water rises up our legs
and we draw close
to the wooden rail,
talking away the hours
to keep from falling in.

STREAM

Trickling through the reeds
in the wispy dawn,
a stream has run for miles
in circuits in my arms
and inlets of my body,
depositing silt
in hidden basins.
So most of us die
from too much or too little
of something—mud,
sunlight, moon—anything
that casts its spell
across the water.
Outside, curtains of cloud
draw closed, and bunchgrass
kicks in the foothills.
I lie in bed
sensing the stream
bending within.
Perhaps my old self
still sits on the banks—
Here, cattails spiral
in starred constellations
and the stream passes near,
snapping its wrists at mayflies
before turning back
to the narrows.

Yet I think I'm not done,
I've not had enough
of dusk's dark skin
on my own
and not enough sunsets
streaking red rouge
on my hands,
over the roads and front porch
and peeling wood siding
of the house where I've grown old.
I feel I'm not done
even as a storm
wraps over the roof
and the rock maples sway,
filled up with spirit,
drinking their own sugar,
flashing into flame.

SOUTHERN ARIZONA ESCAPE VACATION
Two months after my brother's funeral on 9/10/2001

At dawn I open the windows.
Ravens hunch on streetlamps
so naturally they seem

ancient as desert rock.
Scavenging dumpsters
for food, they toss themselves

like raincoats over the lights.
You sleep as I step outside
our sun-faded motel

the rent-a-car ticking
in Western time.
Last night we clung

like the Tohono O'odham
to a bare neck of the land,
curled in the crook of its arm.

This time of year
it's hard to believe
in a few months

the desert will turn green—
spirals of ocotillo, saguaro,
prickly pear like a mime's hands

overflowing with blossoms.
But today we'll be tourists,
gathering canyon dust

under our shoes.
We'll wander the town
and think about moving

to a land without water.
And perhaps
my brother's spirit will follow

for the brief unfurling of spring.
I watch the horizon's smile
breaking with conifers,

the sunrise bruises up blue
and ravens ink up our day
at the base of the Huachuca mountains.

IV

MY FIRST JOB

I trace electrical schematics
at a computer terminal, luminous
in monochrome, turn

a pencil sharpener's
manual crank handle—
The scent of pencil shavings

always reminds me
of a sweater after a rain,
of slick streets beyond

Thanksgiving, when the mature
maples droop
red hair along their branches.

Just out of school,
my desk is strewn
with gum wrappers, coins,

unsent letters home.
Despite San Diego's
sun-plump afternoons

its ocean sunsets
the color of blush wine,
I miss eastern seasons,

snowfall in my lap,
the swish of a winter coat
when you remove the clasp.

And arms of frost
reaching around windows,
air sifting under doors

into the furnace.
When I finally call
our conversation cracks

with spidery lightning
from thunderstorms back east.
So I quit, piling books, papers, memos

on my desk. Flying back,
I drink in one last sunset—
my old life's light

clinging to my my lips
as the plane banks east
below the citrus moon.

IN THE DARK

Doctors gaze at Mom's CAT scan
the way astronomers look
between galaxies.
For space is mostly dark
like our old staircase
where I'd turn
by the dim-lit landing,
angling to the last step
past my brother's closed door.
Once he didn't make the turn,
winding up on the roof—
legs over gutters
among boughs
swaying like drunken angels.
The last day I see Mom
in the memory ward
she has forgotten him,
so I finally sign the form
withholding antibiotics,
closing a door
my brother and I
crawled through.

She stayed a year in this place
with only one floor, not taking steps
in a wheelchair. Back at the house
the stairs seem more slippery,
full of blind turns,
winding upward and outward.
For no one knows what's beyond
roof and chimney,
leaf litter and acorns—
Here a person might sit
beside squirrels and owls,
transfixed by the vastness,
remaining entirely unseen,
caught in a loose gauze
of the stars.

VERTIGO

I scroll through Kim Novak's webpage
of paintings—butterflies and elves
in pastel, on misted boughs.

Just below, her self-portrait
as she once was—hair drawn tight,
shaped in a question mark

as any women would, planning
to disappear. Despite her story
on the page, I can't forget

her transformation in the movie—
returning in straight brown hair,
a plain pleated dress, disguised

as her own self.
Perhaps she reminded me of you,
married and returned.

The movie, too, was in limbo,
trapped in Hitchcock's estate—
its skyblue celluloid frames

fading in a drawer, metal reels
rattling with unease, like branches
on the windows.

When we finally met, we could see
in each other, seasons brighten
and fade. So we watched

the movie again
and the same story unwound—
down spiral streets, steep

as double helices—a city's
staircase of DNA—
concrete, grass, sun.

So the plot unfurled
whispered and slow
as if it were you and I

on the avenues and esplanades,
in cafes and porticoes
in a story not our own.

Yet we could never understand
each scene, or the mystery
of the end—Even after

I took you to the airport,
on the way home,
I had this feeling of falling

before I fell—
of the ground rising up,
turquoise sky above.

POISON IVY

This year, it's everywhere,
flinging woody wrists
around necks of oaks.

Hungry grackles soon arrive,
gathering in the yard
while inside

our cat looks on,
tail twitching. Last week
he must have prowled

and rubbed the poison leaves—
Holding him caused blisters
on my lips and arms.

Wherever he brushed
August wrote its name
in streaks of red.

Once in the bath,
he cried and clawed. Scratches
cross-hatched over wheals.

With a shot of cortisone
spreading in my hip,
I grabbed a sprayer

aiming herbicide
into the trees.
I'm cautious now

on button-down summer nights.
The grackles shift uneasily,
the cat goes on a prowl.

I plump his blanket,
knowing he'll return,
that the ivy will creep back

this year or next, hiding tiny berries
beneath unfaithful blooms
all across the lawn.

WHEN YOU WERE A LIBRARIAN

You traced fingers
over the worn leather covers

of the History Of The Civil War,
Vol I, then along the railroad tracks

of its spine, gingerly
following broken ties,

chipped rails.
As plumes of engine steam,

musket fire,
gleamed again

in the library darkness,
I wondered if your hands

would melt the glue
that binds all history, page by page,

the way a man is bound
—his spine weathered, standing

unread and unspoken.
You looked up, into my skin

where the corpses
of confederate nerves stirred again.

Then you looked down,
returned to your work—

For a librarian's task is endless,
stacking books like grain

sorting and plowing
information in a flickering screen.

And I watched your right hand
graze the keyboard

while your left hand sifted
through the gilt-edged, half-
open pages of your hair.

ELEGY FOR LYN LIFSHIN
R.I.P. 2019

You wrote easily
as fireflies making light.
A poem for every grassblade

in my summer lawn
and one in every magazine—
mainstream to xeroxed.

You'd slip into print
with short, tense lines
and stanzas like stained

broken glass—sharp
enough to nick skin
or slit down to the bone.

Book by book,
your words
grew before me.

Widely read, almost
ubiquitous, you even appeared
in Rolling Stone, yet always

with the same photo—
scoured by dust and film grain,
as if a 70s street scene

overlaid your languorous hair.
Autumn by autumn, boughs
caught fire—like fuses

lit to your last winter.
Perhaps you left
on what you loved—

A horse, tail flicking
in a river,
water rising up its rippled flanks

and delicate black legs
as it took you to the other side.
Now your bones lie hungry

among the stones and tubers
in the black loam of New York.
Only the ink of words remains—

in books on shelves,
by coffee cups and dust,
glowing on the web in L.E.D.

But your spirit lingers,
diffuse as twilight
on these Kentucky evenings

when my lawn's sequined
in fireflies. So I read your book
beneath the sugar maples

watching as the fireflies flash
and rise, all through June
into the continuous night.

PERFUME

Take essences of things.
Like lime with its skin's light
of sheer green fields.
Or the scent
of damp forgotten earth.
Sweeten with wild rose
and frail hyacinth, tied
with its own laces on April lawns.
Perfume should be worldly,
spiced by trade-winds,
fixed in ambergris—
The sea's gray seed,
taken by ocean breezes
past shipwreck, over storm-wrack,
beached up and trapped
in a skin of glass.
Because we're old,
longitude and latitude
have swept across our faces,
with each crease a journey back,
a delineation of desire
where anyplace could be a waypoint
or destination—
So take coconut, flesh and hull.
Fray corn silk, fragile
as riggings of telephone lines
across the boughs
beside our window.
Add one tendril
of sea foam off of rock.
Create perfume
to fill the mind,
swell the body's sails, and sway
your auburn hair.

ICE STORM 2021

1.

In February
winter pressed its burden
of cold into us.

We could feel winter's heartbeat
— sleet, rain, ice—
ticking on roofs and windows.

A bitter wind
fell south, a drunken breath
seeped in cracks

of the house.
By morning
barns broke under

the weight of snow,
black ribs poking through
the ice.

Power lines unraveled,
torn like kite string,
the electricity was out for days.

After that,
arguing, hungry, trapped—
nothing was the same.

2.

Forgiveness comes
with spring revivals
of green clasped buds, opening—

with brash violets
and impulsive phlox
running over the fields.

So past splintered limbs
and snowmelt, I turn
my car's wheels down rte. 27

crossing the spindly legs
of a country road
up to your home.

Through the window,
fences comb a pasture's hair,
cows low in meditation.

I hope to see you soon—
lift your necklaces
of ice, your earrings

of crystal cold.
For you are
a winter sky

your skin, a migration
of freckles
lit by the distant horizon—

Here cold and warm entwine,
light thatches cloud
and sun strikes earth

to breaking. For our future
is our fate—of light and heat
beyond all reckoning.

THE TIDES
Portland Oregon, 1970

Crouching at my grandmother's
dressing room door,
I watch her comb her hair

layered like silver pines.
She dabs on rouge
the color of an Oregon sunrise

just below the tungsten
filaments of her eyes.
Visiting next year

her eyesight's full of clouds.
We bring her from the hospital
bandaged after cataracts

needing two weeks in bed,
so I prowl the house unseen—
past tables of coral, china,

by a bowl of scalloped soap
scented fuchsia, rose
as if from her hillside garden

where I first gazed at Mt. Hood,
St. Helens, The Three Sisters in white veils
of mist and distance.

With bones seabird-thin,
I stoop in her dressing room's
secluded cove

and pick her earrings up
like agates
we would gather

at Sauvie's island.
Swaying in the current,
I steal into her closet

and slide her favorite dress
sheer as a summer evening
on my shoulders.

For a moment, I become her—
a woman at the ocean's edge,
not seeing but feeling

every movement of the water
where I reach
into a furrow in the tides.

PORTRAIT OF TIME AS AN OLD WOMAN

Portland, Oregon, 1973

Cradling a decanter
—cut sapphire crystal—

my grandmother would pour sherry,
rosining my vocal cords.

She'd paint calamine
like milk across welts

of poison sumac on my arms.
I was twelve and out of school

when jazz dropped
on the console stereo

and the needle fell into the groove
July nights.

Music lifted through the hall
as I lay in bed

while her hands slid down my neck
like fingers on the banisters.

Now when I walk
on floral carpets,

past fleur-de-lis covered walls,
I find that hugging her

is like grasping a vase of lilacs,
stems thin and brittle,

that she's fragile as the rim
of an old L.P. And all I hear

is the warning groove
at record's end,
ticking off and on
like steady breathing,

as if she's asking to be turned
to the other side.

THINGS I KEEP NEAR

I keep a notebook by the bed—
its pages like empty fields
strung with green wires
where I hope words alight,
flown out of sleep.
But the grasses blow empty,
the book's never opened.
Beside it on the nightstand
is an antique jar—a gift
from my grandmother
which still holds
her evaporated tears,
grown diamond-hard
as grit in my eyes
when I wake, dried and old.
And in a pillowcase
under your head,
I hid a lock of your hair
that spilled in my hands
in a trove of black coins
when we met.
Tonight's our October
anniversary—

The Halloween moon
shines toothy side down
in the grass, the air's
spiced with orange rinds
and nutmeg and clove
from your skin. Again I lie down
in the dark cloud of your hair
like taking a midnight train
into November's distances—
through cold grasses and thin rains,
sloping valleys and curled-up hills,
its whistle ringing
in a night full of dreams.

CAMPING AT NIGHT

As nestling birds shiver
in billowing trees,
we tuck in a sleeping bag
where I feel feathers
on the edge of my skin.
Next day at a waterfall
you unravel
each watery strand, slipping
away like a part of yourself
which will never return,
while on the way down,
you trace a seep on the shale
cliff where I stand, still
as a mossy stone in your palm.
We drive back
to your high-rise apartment
and lie in the space
between two semesters,
listening to pipes in the walls
roil with water and rust.

We don't understand—
camping is luck
so we let summer drag on
and its humid haze sticks
to the roof like a tongue
slipping into September,
to skies of monarchs
like flecks of stained glass.
When you graduate and leave
I sit on our steps
watching December tinge gray—
The cold seeps in
the sky like a bruise
and starlings and blackbirds
flock dense as blackberry vines,
wings tangled up,
rasping and singing,
each one a nestling
grown fast, in flight.

VINES

1. Looking At Your X-Rays

Viral proteins tumble
past an inner garden edge
like dandelions blowing
through wet fences of your ribs.

Blood vessels, like dogwoods
that normally bloom in pink,
transform to leafless limbs.
And deeper, in the world

of your body—
pulsing rivers, sweeping culverts,
swales and basins
in unseen spaces

where air should flow
fill with viral snow.
I think you won't return
once they check you in.

2. Home Alone

I prowl the yard
under clotheslines
where you hung our shirts
like second selves

cuffs dangling in air.
Past hollies to the garden shed.
Here a wood stove molders—
iron claw feet anchored

in soft wood, a chimney choked
by bird nests, branches—
This is your spirit
turned to iron.

Sometimes it wheezes
when the wind picks up,
speaking as you might
from your sickbed—

orange sparks
of fever on your breath,
viral cinders on your tongue
and as you breathe

a breeze drifts in the stove's
rusted gut, searching
ash, burnt sticks,
for the hidden, wavering flame.

3. The Return

I sit porchside, one cat
on each porch stone,
waiting for your hands.
When you arrive

I help you up the steps.
Plague surges
in a blizzard, while at home,
mid-morning calm—

dew hanging in bracelets
on wisteria and ivy.
Our cats sprawl on garden tiles,
licking grass-soft fur

then their paws,
to disinfect and heal,
rasped tongues swirling
layers of whiteness

thick as my throat
on seeing you again—
as pale and sweet
as clotted cream.

4. Dis-enchantment

Two weeks home,
the laundry flaps
on its own, the woodstove
breathes, wooden beams

inside our house tick even
when we're gone.
Nothing is as it was.
Plague mutates in a storm

and all summer we're confined
as the ivy grows
up walls, chimneys—
a sinewy vine

latching on as we do,
in a tightening spiral,
each leaf edge
tangling the days.

As we cook and clean in solitude
ivy crawls the roof.
This high, swallows flit
in spaces between branches

like spirits of the dead.
And each night
we think about mortality,
watching streetlights sidle

by the window, casting circles
in our hair. A familiar rush
of wings, talons scraping gutters
as the swallows fold

gray feathers, settling to rest
like layers of the day,
closing onto dust
in temples of the eaves

DECEMBER ARABESQUE

Before spiked seed pods
and berets of acorns
like buried in drifts,

before winter singes
thick-fingered shrubs,
I grab a broom, bucket and rag.

Sweeping the blacktop
down to the stubble,
I drag fallen leaves

in a bag, wipe the glaze
of frost from my window,
cleaning the steps

in case you return.
When I look up,
it seems like the day

you first came back—sky
cloudy-white, bearing handfuls
of mutable weather.

That night you brought
winter's bare limbs, layered in ice,
a necklace of snow

draped on the pale horizon
by my drawn window.
Here your body unwound

while winter's clothing piled up,
its cold ground spreading for miles,
curtained in white, freckled by crows.

86

CALLED HOME

I tasted the tang
of lead paint off the garage
where I learned to dribble and shoot,
practicing until the basketball
folded its wings into my palm.
I breathed in cleaner
Mom used in the bathroom—
a distillation of pine forests
and tree shadow.
I took things into my body
that would never leave,
carrying them with me,
visiting after she died.
In the backyard—
months of rain
turned to dandelions
along the rear boundary
where I'd slip under a chain link fence,
walking to an abandoned coal pile,
past the iron spines
of railroad tracks,
by thickets of pipe vine,
wild grape, hemlock
and thistles that wore
violet eyeshadow all summer.
From that far place
Mom called me home, her voice
echoing over the driveway
through the lot next door,
to the rusty fence,
then to my ears
and fields beyond.

NOTES

Thanks to the Arts Center of The Bluegrass in Danville, Kentucky for sponsoring Poetry Connected. "Mystic Owl" and "Moving Colors" are ekphrastic poems written for these exhibitions.

Thanks to Natalie Marino for looking over many of these poems and for her suggestions and inspiring examples.

Thanks to the Lexington-Frankfort writer's group, for a decade of help (Jeff Worley, Marica Hurlow, Richard Taylor, Mike Moran, Karen Osborn, David Youngblood, Tom Webster, Lance Olsen, Leatha Kendrick, Susan Cobin, Jo Leadingham, Kenny King and George Ella Lyon).
Thanks to the Kentucky Arts Council for a generous Al Smith Fellowship in 2008 and for sponsoring Poetry Connected.

ABOUT THE AUTHOR

David Cazden has lived in Kentucky for over 50 years and is currently a resident of Boyle County. He was the poetry editor for Miller's Pond magazine for five years and a finalist for the Pablo Neruda Award (Nimrod International magazine). He received an Al Smith Fellowship for poetry from the Kentucky Arts Council.

www.ingramcontent.com/pod-product-compliance
Lightning Source LLC
Chambersburg PA
CBHW051639120626
46551CB00014B/2136